WHEN A CITY LEANS AGAINST THE SKY

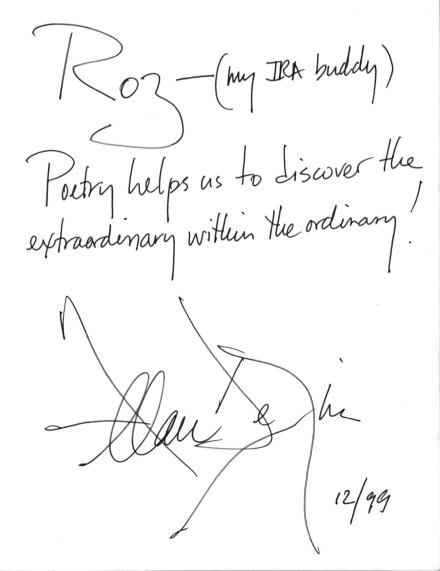

Roz — (my IRA buddy)

Poetry helps us to discover the extraordinary within the ordinary!

12/99

WHEN A CITY LEANS AGAINST THE SKY

Poems by Allan A. De Fina

Illustrations by Ken Condon

WORDSONG
BOYDS MILLS PRESS

Published by Wordsong
Boyds Mills Press, Inc.
A Highlights Company
815 Church Street
Honesdale, Pennsylvania 18431
Printed in Mexico

Publisher Cataloging-in-Publication Data
De Fina, Allan A..
    When a city leans against the sky / by Allan A. De Fina ; illustrated by Ken
Condon.—1st ed.
[64]p. : col.ill. ; cm.
Summary : A collection of poems about life in the city.
ISBN 1-56397-137-2
1. City and town life—Children's poetry. [1. City and town life—Poetry.]
I. Condon, Ken, ill. II. Title.
811.54—dc20   1997   AC   CIP
Library of Congress Catalog Card Number 94-79159

First edition, 1997
Book designed by Tim Gillner and Gordon Tin
The text of this book is set in 14-point Clearface.
The illustrations are done in pencil.

10 9 8 7 6 5 4 3

CONTENTS:

WHEN A CITY LEANS
AGAINST THE SKY 7
STORIES 8

CITY STREETS
CITY BUS 10
TAXIS 11
RAINY MORNING 12
WET CITY 13
SUMMER VACATION 14
SUMMER ICICLES 15
SKYSCRAPER CLIMBER 16
SNOWY MORNING 17
ZIPPER 18

CITY SIGHTS
TRAPPED CITY 20
SHADOWS 21
FIRE ESCAPE PRINCESS 22
CITY ZOO 23
HARBOR 24
BRIDGE 25
SCHEDULED CROSSINGS 26
SUNSET LIGHTING 28

ABOVE GROUND
COMPANY 30
BEWARE! 31
PARK BENCH 32
PLAYGROUND 33
SUNDAY CITY 34
STORM 35

WEB 36
MONUMENTS 37
EMPTY PLAYGROUND 38

UNDERGROUND
UNDERGROUND 40
RIDING THE SUBWAY TRAIN 41
DRAGON BELOW! .42
SUBWAY MAP 43
THE CAVERN 44

CITY PEOPLE
KALEIDOSCOPE 46
CITY STRUT 47
INVISIBLE CITY 48
REFLECTIONS 49
BACKS 50
STOP-AND-GO GAME 51
CITY COWBOY 52
AT THE HOT DOG CAFÉ 53
HARD HATS 54
UNSEEN CITY 55
BEDTIME READING .56

CITY SKIES
UNDER CONSTRUCTION 58
SKY SCRAPING 59
LIGHTNING 60
LOOKING OUT FROM THE EIGHTEENTH FLOOR 61
EMPIRE STATE BUILDING 62
CHESS MOVES 63
SLEEPY CITY 64

WHEN A CITY LEANS AGAINST THE SKY

When a city
leans against the sky,
buildings squeeze and
press for elbowroom
with the clouds.
The sky turns blue
and bursts into sun
or moon and stars.

STORIES

Only a city
has more stories
behind each windowed
shelf
than a library
can hold
or a storyteller
tell.

CITY STREETS

CITY BUS

As the bus prowls along
it growls along
and fouls behind.
It scowls with glaring eyes
and strides
between those persons walking by.
It moves its torso
oh, so slow,
scooping strangers
as it goes.

TAXIS

Yellow fireflies
that flicker and flash:
scurrying cabs
madly dash
from corner to corner,
everywhere,
they circle the city
to earn their fare.

Rainy Morning

Sad morning sky—
gray, pigeon gray.
Trees dusted with drizzle
and street lamp light;
store windows darkened,
teasingly echoing
the red-yellow-greens
of nearby traffic lights.
A growling bus
makes a puddle jump
while sleepy traffic
dawdles onto bridges and
yawns into tunnels.
    Here and there
an umbrella
with two legs beneath it
leaps a puddle
and dashes across shiny tar.
The city
never stops running.

WET CITY

After the rain
a wet stain remains
in the

sidewalk gutters,
all aflutter with fallen leaves
and litter.

Long silky rainbows beside concrete
gush flowing puddles
past our feet.

SUMMER VACATION

sun blaring heat
hot wind blowing trumpeted curtains
in sweaty breezes across the
arms and faces hanging out windows
mixed in among the cement layers of red brick
above the potholed streets where
cars slick by between hydrant gushes
and children hopscotch skipping
in and out of fantastic water fountains
improvised by hands
cupping the waterspout
and cupped together—
clapping, celebrating vacation days!

SUMMER ICICLES

open hydrants
silver streamers
frothy white confetti
warm icicles
dangle in ringlets
down foreheads
and drip onto noses
icing up a
summer's day

SKYSCRAPER CLIMBER

Want to climb
to the top of a
skyscraper's peak?

Straddle its
shadow
down sidewalk and street.

SNOWY MORNING

Feather pillow spilling open down
around us white whispers.

The cars that
struggle up the tar streets
leave behind their gray shadows.

ZIPPER

The snow-capped city
wears its white overcoat
this wintry morning.
A solitary taxi cab
opens a zipper
up the avenue.

CITY SIGHTS

TRAPPED CITY

Inside the city's central park
trapped within the lake,
rests the city on its side—
a mirrored double take!

SHADOWS

Beneath the fire escape
piano keys
sparkle in the sunlight.

They make music
only I hear
as I skip my song.

Fire Escape Princess

The cat on the window sill,
a fire escape princess,
directs the traffic
at her address.

To the streets below
she gives a glance,
commanding trucks and cabs
to stop their dance.

Both paws outstretched,
she beckons a sunbeam,
tunes out the city
and dreams royal dreams.

CITY ZOO

There are animals loose in the city zoo—
though the animals think
there are people loose who

surround them and feed them
and photograph them, too!

HARBOR

The harbor is alone this morning,
not even a gull or tug
to keep time with its waves.
Damp and heavy ropes
dangle at empty moorings
as old wooden piers
creak and groan.
Finally the sun
lays a carpet across the bay.
But still, no one ventures out.
The city is slow to start its day.

BRIDGE

The gray bridge
castles into the night sky
and leaves its ghostly etchings
of steel columns and cables there

It holds apart two shores
while furious headlighted cars
skip back-and-forth across the
broken white lines

SCHEDULED CROSSINGS

The ferry
slips into the sea-green fog
with a yellow-misted glow and
skips above white-hatted waves
from one corner of the island
toward the invisible city.

It trails its lights
across the bay;
its horn sings its name
within the gray.

Slowly,
the eyes of the city
begin to open
and search the waters;
a chorus of cabs and
newspaper hawkers call the ferry
from the lint-lined night
to the shore.

Soon the ferry
hugs the terminal
(wearing the night
and neon shadows)
as it heaves and rests
before once again
scraping into the hollow
of the fog.

Sunset Lighting

The red sunset folds up
across the city's frame

while watercolor blues
wash down darkness.

Streets torch with lamplight
and neon streams

rush and
bounce on river tops.

ABOVE GROUND

COMPANY

What strange company
statues keep:
pigeons
at both head and feet!

BEWARE!

Revolving door
gulps one more;
eats up people,
hungry carnivore!

PARK BENCH

park bench
parked bench
benched park

in the middle
of the city
waiting for passers-by

PLAYGROUND

under the green lace fire escape iron
suspended perches
descending, climbing, scaling
the gray black sides
of the big apartment hideouts.
No sun,

but noise
television jingles
and laundry lines
measure the box alley perimeter

where a little boy plays
with his gray cat with
white stripes and yellow,
sometimes green, eyes.

SUNDAY CITY

Sleepy city
slumbers still,
Sunday stretching slowly.
Sunrise scrawling signatures on
silent streets and sidewalks;
sky and subway
sneaking softly, shade and
shush the sounds of
Sunday stirring.

Storm

The storm waits
above the city spires;
clouds mass and cover
shiny silver skyscrapers
fade to gray and
crimson glass loses its glow.

Below, the shadowed streets
lose the edges of the skyline
and dim to the color of clouds.

Droplets gather
and pelt the earth.
Where they land
umbrellas sprout!

WEB

How incredible!
A sun-kissed spider
has spun its rainbow threads
Across a skyscraper's windowpanes!

MONUMENTS

Church graveyards
in the shadows
of skyscrapers:

Stone monuments
lost in the gray of
other stone monuments.

EMPTY PLAYGROUND

Silent chalk hopscotch boxes
and fading asphalt love letters,
empty swings and netless basketball hoops.
Cold winds blow through wire fences
and roll a hollow can.
No voices echo here today
as winter claims its turf.

UNDERGROUND

UNDERGROUND

silver subway star
streaking snakelike
sneaking, snarling

crackling in caverns
crouching, crooning,
cackling, coughing

people poised, pondering,
posing, primping
preparing

a new day outside
the dark tunnels

Riding the Subway Train

Hurrying, hustling, hurtling past,
the subway train
approaches at last!

Whooshing, whizzing, whistling air,
blows in faces
and messes hair!

Rumble, rattle, screeching stop!
The train rolls in,
and on all hop.
Snap! Shut! Train doors close!
It jerks and lurches
as off it goes!

Whooshing, whizzing, whistling along!
The subway sings
its noisy song.

DRAGON BELOW!

There's a dragon under the
city streets—
who thrashes about
and stamps his feet.

I feel his rumble
and hear his roar.
Buildings tremble
to the highest floor!

He snorts his anger
in bursts of steam;
through sidewalk holes
his fury screams!

There's something wild
loose below—
and I'm not waiting here
to see him show!

SUBWAY MAP

Colored veins
lace the map,
arteries
that overlap
and trace
the city's pace below,
its beating life line's
constant flow.

THE CAVERN

Stalactites meet stalagmites
down the subway tunnel.
Subway stanchions hold the black
within the darkened funnel.

Through the scrambling stations,
train cars scrape and move,
while deeply in the cavern
howl the whistling wind-wolves.

Spark and clack against the track,
cave creatures rush to flight,
scattered by the sounds and stirs
that scratch the pitch-black light.

CITY PEOPLE

KALEIDOSCOPE

Rainbow colors
of vibrant faces,
city people
of many races.
Voices dance
with different songs,
different music
from varied tongues.
All together
in one place,
a sparkling kaleidoscope
of the human race!

CITY STRUT

The people in the city walk
in an awful hurry.
They never stop to look about.
All they do is scurry!

INVISIBLE CITY

He leans
against a building
that isn't there
and walks on a sidewalk
that rolls beneath him.
He picks flowers
and eats fruit he takes
from invisible markets.
And he presses his nose up
against big windows
and pushes heavy doors.
How much more to the city
there is than I can see!
The man with the white make-up face
sees it all!

Reflections

Tens of thousands of people
walking by
shiny store windows
multiply:
Twenties of thousands of people
walking by!

BACKS

In the elevator,
in back of backs!
On the escalator,
ankle backs!
City sidewalks,
marching backs!
City people
have no faces!

STOP-AND-GO GAME

Crowds of children
WALK/DON'T WALK
on their way to class.

"Mother, may I?"
children ask
before they cross at last.

CITY COWBOY

I want to ride
the quarter horse
in front of the
five-and-dime store.

I don't dare
ask my mom because
I'm not a kid
anymore.

AT THE HOT DOG CAFÉ

Hot dog man
beneath the umbrella,
wrapped in warm
steam and sauerkraut smells.

Hands in pockets,
he waits by his cart,
"Franks with mustard,
a dollar," he yells.

Cool winter noontime,
his corner café
bustles with business
as lunches he sells.

HARD HATS

Balanced on beams
across the sky,
hard hats hurdle
steel towers high.
Like pigeons perched
on building ledges,
construction workers
touch cloud edges.

UNSEEN CITY

Voices echo
beneath the street,
heads pop up
among our feet.
What goes on
down below
where all the hard-hat
workers go?

BEDTIME READING

Where do you think
the man
in the newspaper hut sleeps?

Do you think he
tosses and turns
on magazine heaps?

For a pillow
does he use
the latest edition
of the news?

CITY SKIES

UNDER CONSTRUCTION

Steel bones—
museum dinosaurs
escape outdoors into
   the sunlight,
necks held high
above the brick and glass
   of surrounding mountains,
peering over the horizon,
slowly becoming part of
   the cityscape
as they become extinct.

SKY SCRAPING

Clouds snap their bottoms
on skyscraper tops,
and spill out their insides
in little sun drops.

LIGHTNING

Against the skyline
the veins in the neck of the sky
are showing.

Thunderously,
the sky pounds its fists
on rooftops.

Looking Out From the Eighteenth Floor

The rain stitches the windowpane.
Its zippered stripes
zigzag across the city's face—
a connect-the-dots
imposed upon the gray skyline.

Perhaps to take a pencil
and sketch in an umbrella
where the sky meets the spires.

EMPIRE STATE BUILDING

Bright yellow moon
pinned to the needle
of the Empire State Building
giant birthday candle